Unforgettable Neighbours

BY ANNA WING-BO TSO
ILLUSTRATED BY JOANNE WAI-NAM LO

Dedication

From Anna Wing-bo Tso: I dedicate this book to the treasured memory of my grannies, Mr and Mrs James Tso, who are always remembered with love. This book is also fondly dedicated to my brothers, Andrew and Angus. I hold a special place in my heart for you both.

From Joanne : To my parents, Johnny and Connie, my brother Jessie, who have made my childhood an amazing journey, and for spoiling me to remain a dreamer and a creative artist.

Acknowledgements

The Hong Kong Stories series has been substantially funded by a project grant from the Sunrise Charitable and Education Fund (reference no.: S/V/EL in U001 (8/2016)).

Foreword

This series of Hong Kong-based children's stories amalgamate inventive adventure, dynamism, commotion and tightly bound collective memories, providing a pleasurable reading in English full of amusement, significance and reminiscence not only to Hong Kong readers but also to those from far and wide.

Unforgettable Neighbours, book 3 of the children's picture book project, tells the story of three siblings - Andrew, Anna and Angus - who get together for a hike on the southern coast of Tung Ping Chau in Hong Kong. Under a starry night, the trio recollects memorable situations during the period they lived with their grannies in the Belcher's Gardens - a place where they used to welcome families and friends and bump into some uninvited mates like Sir Gigantic Spider and Mr. Fruit Bat. Even their mom spotted once a Lady King Cobra in Belcher's concrete path up the hill. Hair-raising, isn't it? Such scary episodes are the connecting bond between these sibs and the readers of this book will definitely also fall for the colourful images of Tung Ping Chau's topography and the Belcher's wealth of fauna and flora. Due to encounters with such "unforgettable neighbours", this Hong Kong animal safari makes Andrew, Anna and Angus miss the past dreadfully, "Gone were the good old days", recalls Andrew. Despite having pictures and situations locked in their hearts and minds, these grown-ups - already in their thirties - can contemplate these mind-blowing events as blessings from heaven. As Tom Stoppard remarked once, "If you carry your childhood with you, you never become older".

I feel confident to say that *Unforgettable Neighbours* is a stupendous addition to the juvenile literary world and will attain all the honours it deserves!

Flowery greetings, from The Netherlands
Claudia dos Santos Cunha, MA in Applied English Linguistics
at the Open University of Hong Kong (2012-2013)
Currently Teacher of Portuguese at the Volksuniversiteit, Den Haag,
The Netherlands

"When was the last time the three of us sat together and talked in a cloudless night?" Anna asked.

After a whole day of hiking along the wave-cut shore on the southern coast of Tung Ping Chau, the three siblings – Andrew, Anna, and Angus rested outside the tent they built shortly before dusk. They had just finished their BBQ supper and were enjoying iced beer under the starry night. Andrew and Angus had left Hong Kong for Australia since their secondary school graduation. Now, all three of them were already in their thirties. They worked in different cities and had a family of their own. It was not easy for them to get together in Hong Kong. Going hiking in Tung Ping Chau was Anna's idea.

Named after **Sir Edward Belcher**, a British naval officer and explorer, Belcher's Gardens was built in 1958 in the Western Mid-levels area of Hong Kong Island. Before it was demolished in the 1990s and redeveloped as high-rise residential apartments, the serene villa was surrounded by a wealth of greenery, private gardens, antique ponds, fountains and playgrounds. For almost 40 years, it was their grannies' home sweet home.

Andrew, Anna and Angus had lived several years with their grannies too before moving out with their parents. Although the Belcher's Gardens was no more and their grannies had left many years ago, it was a sanctuary of the heart where collective memories were shared.

"Yes, the last time we had a chat under the cloudless night was during our night stroll at the Belcher's Gardens, which was, I am afraid, twenty years ago at least!" How did time go by so quickly? Anna was lost in thought.

"The Belcher's was fantastic in every way, and you know, we had some fantastic mates too." Angus winked his eye.
"You mean, the Ng's family and the Wong's family?" Andrew asked, raising his right eyebrow.

"Certainly they were nice guys, and besides, we had a fantastic ROOMMATE, Sir Gigantic Spider who always hid in grandpa's studio. He loved books I bet, haha." Angus couldn't hold his laughter back.

"Oh yes, he was bigger than my head! I'm glad that he was a shy peacemaker, not an aggressive face-hanger." Andrew chuckled. "And do you remember Mr. Fruit Bat? One evening before dinner, he flew into our grannies' dining room uninvitedly. I knew he came for the ripe bananas on the ancestor shrine, but his flappy wings were a bit too frightening. We kids were so scared that we all hid under the table."

"Mom said one fine afternoon as she was returning home from work, she saw a stout grey snake of 2m who proudly slithered cross the hilly road in front of her. In the blink of an eye, the snake disappeared into a car that parked at the roadside. That car belonged to Mr. Wong, our neighbour. Mom was worried so she called the security guard, who then called Mr. Wong about the case, as well as the snake master in the neighbourhood." Angus had a good memory of all incidents that happened in childhood.

"But why didn't they call the cops?" Anna wondered.
"That's because Lady King Cobra would become the snake master's pet if she was caught, whereas if they called the cops, the caught wild animal may be killed."

Angus continued the rest of the story, "When the snake master arrived, he checked Mr. Wong's car carefully, tapped on all sides of the car, but still he could not hear anything nor see Lady King Cobra's shadow. Where was she hiding? The only hiding place was, of course, beneath the bonnet.

When the snake master lifted the bonnet, they found that Lady King Cobra was all coiled up and ready to strike! In the split of a second, the snake master caught the snake in the neck and threw it inside a big rice bag. Lady King Cobra kept rolling and rolling inside the bag, but there was no escape. Lady King Cobra was tamed at last."

"Our old neighbours were surely unforgettable. Gone were the good old days."
Andrew finished his beer.

"Let's get some sleep before we watch the sunrise tomorrow, shall we?" They all missed the Belcher's too much.

Sometimes, sweet memories can become bitter too if you miss them too much.

Anna went back to the tent to prepare the sleeping bags. That night, all three of the brothers and sister dreamt about their grannies and their old home.

Book series author

Anna Wing-bo Tso is an associate professor of English and Comparative Literature at The Open University of Hong Kong. Interested in children's literature, gender studies, language arts and translation studies, Anna has organized numerous international conferences in her areas of expertise and published research articles in peer-reviewed journals across Asia, Europe, the U.K., the U.S., Canada, Australia and New Zealand. She is the author of the *Hong Kong Stories* series (Alpha Academic Press, 2017 -), the first author of *Academic Writing for Arts and Humanities Students* (McGraw-Hill, 2016), the co-author of *Teaching Shakespeare to ESL Students* (Springer, 2017), and the associate editor of Springer's *Digital Culture and Humanities* book series. In her free time, she also writes and publishes plays, poems, short stories, and children's picture books for leisure. Her prose and verse have appeared in literary periodicals and national newspapers, including *The Font, American Tanka, New Academia,* and *China Times*.

Book series illustrator

Joanne Lo was born in Canada and raised both in Toronto and Hong Kong. Having grown up and living on a beautiful outlying island called Cheung Chau, she has a special love for nature, animals, art and one's spiritual growth. She began her career in creative media since graduating from university majoring in Cultural Studies and Visual Studies. She is the illustrator of *Teaching Shakespeare to ESL Students* (Springer, 2017), a book housed in the Yale and Harvard University Libraries and downloaded for over 7,860 times since its publication. As a favour for young readers, she is working on a funded children's book series about Hong Kong memories.

Hong Kong Stories
The Complete Series

Tailor-made for young readers at ages 8 - 12 in Hong Kong and beyond, the *Hong Kong Stories* series is a collection of English stories written with the local Hong Kong context in mind. Ideal for language learning, leisure and reading aloud among readers young and old, the book series will bring together original short stories and pictures about various aspects of Hong Kong's everyday life:

Book 1: *Culinary Charades*, a taster of Hong Kong food
Book 2: *The Summer of 1997*, a walk down memory lane in HK
Book 3: *Unforgettable Neighbours*, a Hong Kong animal safari
Book 4: *Taming Babel*, the serendipity of the Cantonese language
Book 5: *Herstory*, a tribute to Hong Kong women
Book 6: *A Tale of Two Haunted Universities*, a spooky Halloween treat

www.ingramcontent.com/pod-product-compliance
Lightning Source LLC
Chambersburg PA
CBHW041215240426
43661CB00012B/1050